C000016354

Did Yo

WORC

Compiled by Julia Skinner
With particular reference to the work of B Abraham and Julie Meech

THE FRANCIS FRITH COLLECTION

www.francisfrith.com

Based on a book first published in the United Kingdom in 2006 by The Francis Frith Collection®

This edition published exclusively for Bradwell Books in 2012
For trade enquiries see: www.bradwellbooks.com or tel: 0800 834 920
ISBN 978-1-84589-402-3

British Library Cataloguing in Publication Data

Did You Know? Worcester - A Miscellany
Compiled by Julia Skinner
With particular reference to the work of B Abraham and Julie Meech

The Francis Frith Collection
Oakley Business Park,
Wylye Road, Dinton,
Wiltshire SP3 5EU
Tel: +44 (0) 1722 716 376
Email: info@francisfrith.co.uk
www.francisfrith.com

Printed and bound in Malaysia
Contains material sourced from responsibly managed forests

Front Cover: **WORCESTER, THE CROSS 1923** 73755p

The colour-tinting is for illustrative purposes only, and is not intended to be historically accurate

CONTENTS

INTRODUCTION

There has been a settlement at Worcester for over 2,000 years, as numerous Iron Age finds indicate. It owes its origin to the River Severn, which was fordable at this point at low tide, making it the only crossing place between Gloucester and Bridgnorth, and therefore of both practical and strategic importance. In the late 7th century Worcester acquired a cathedral and the town became an increasingly important religious centre, with the wealth of the church acting as a stimulus for commerce. Worcester prospered throughout the medieval period. The community engaged in an enormous variety of trades and crafts, and traded with France, Germany, Spain, Iceland and the Low Countries.

Cloth and clothing manufacture came to dominate the economy and the city acquired an international reputation for its products. Worcester became a Royalist garrison during the Civil War, and in 1646 it withstood three months of siege before surrendering to the Parliamentary forces. During the siege some medieval suburbs were deliberately destroyed by the garrison to prevent the Parliamentarians from approaching too close to the city walls, and further massive damage took place during the Battle of Worcester in 1651, so it is not surprising that the city has few surviving medieval buildings.

In the 18th and 19th centuries the city was heavily dependant on its declining clothing industries, particularly glove making, and a huge underclass lived in great poverty in the city's slums. It was partly to reduce unemployment that in 1751 a group of businessmen founded the Worcester Porcelain Works, and in 1788 a rival firm, Chamberlain & Co, set up on Severn Street. In that same year George III toured the Severn Street works and ordered three dinner services for the royal household. The company received the royal warrant in 1789 and the internationally renowned Royal Worcester Porcelain Company was formed from a merger of the rivals.

Massive redevelopment of the city centre in the 1960s involved the demolition of many of Worcester's remaining ancient buildings. However, the city's medieval street pattern still remains clearly visible, as do stretches of the city walls. The cathedral and the monastic ruins, together with Edgar Tower and the 15th-, 16th- and 17th-century buildings of Friar Street, New Street and Corn Market hint at the glory that was medieval Worcester. There is an abundance of elegant Georgian architecture and some good Victorian buildings too. Despite all that has been lost, Worcester is still a rewarding city to explore. An added attraction is that every third year the city hosts Europe's oldest music festival, the Three Choirs, which it shares with Hereford and Gloucester, and the music of Worcester's most famous son, Sir Edward Elgar, figures in the programme.

WORCESTER, THE MONASTIC RUINS 1891 29307

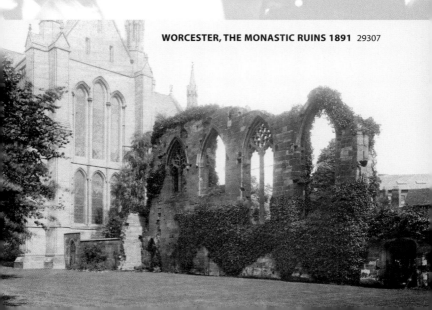

WORCESTERSHIRE WORDS AND PHRASES

'A bit of water' - a drop of water.

'Anant' - against.

'Bibble' - a small stone or a pebble.

'Dummock' - a fool, a stupid person.

'Jaspers' - wasps.

'Jissup' - juice or gravy.

'Mawsy' - over ripe, rotten, as of a fruit or vegetable.

'Mullock' - dirt, a mess.

'Robbled' - tangled, or mixed up.

'Scorkle' - an apple core.

'Scurrock' - a small piece.

'Urchin' - a hedgehog.

'Where bist thee orf to?' - where are you going?

'Yarberin' - yabbering, talking a lot.

'A tom tit on top of a hayrick' - a Worcestershire expression for a small man seen walking with a very large woman.

HAUNTED WORCESTER

The Commandery is one of Worcester's historic buildings. It has a colourful history, and in 2004 two skeletons were found buried beneath what is now the staffroom floor - the bodies are believed to have been buried at the end of the 15th century. The building is said to be one of the most haunted places in Worcester, and strange presences, unexplained cold spots, ghostly apparitions and feelings of terror have been reported by visitors and staff.

The BBC Hereford & Worcester building in Hylton Road was a tannery between 1949 and 1960. A man who worked there at this time and who was suffering from depression is believed to have hanged himself on one of the upper floors after being told off by his boss, and his ghost is said to haunt the building. In 2003 an exorcism was conducted live on air during the Dave Bradley Programme, and during the broadcast many strange noises could be heard.

Since the time of the Civil War, Worcester Cathedral and College Green are said to have been haunted by a phantom bear which rears up as if about to attack, before disappearing into thin air. Ghostly Cavalier and Roundhead soldiers from the Civil War are also said to march through the city's streets at night.

The medium Derek Acorah visited the Worcester Porcelain Museum in Severn Street in 2006, to try to exorcise the spirit of a former apprentice, William Lee, which was said to haunt the building. However, he failed to drive away the spirit - after his visit, staff reported that the ghostly presence could still be felt, and mysterious footsteps could be heard in the gallery he was believed to haunt.

The Battle of Worcester between the forces of Oliver Cromwell and Charles II was fought on September 3rd 1651. Cromwell's forces were chiefly camped in Perry Wood and Red Hill, from where their huge siege cannons had range over the city. Evidence of these encampments, called Cromwell's trenches, can still be seen. Exactly seven years later to the day, on September 3rd 1658, Oliver Cromwell died, during a violent thunderstorm. This gave rise to the legend that Cromwell made a pact with the Devil in Perry Wood, selling his soul in return for a victory and seven more years of his life.

WORCESTER MISCELLANY

Queen Anne, whose statue is above the entrance to the Guildhall, was a most unfortunate woman. She bore at least seventeen children, all of whom died at birth or in childhood. Her reign was one of firsts and lasts: she became the first sovereign of Great Britain when England and Scotland united in 1707; the last one to touch for 'The King's Evil'; and the last to refuse to sign an Act of Parliament.

The Three Choirs Festival is claimed to be Europe's oldest non-competitive choral festival and is hosted in rotation by the cities of Gloucester, Hereford, and Worcester. It began informally early in the 18th century and developed to embrace instrumental as well as choral performances. Until 1837 the gatherings were known as 'meetings', after which the word 'festival' was used. The cathedrals are hired for the occasion by the festival itself.

The British Medical Association was established in Worcester during the 19th century. A local doctor named Charles Hastings, whose home stands opposite the old Gaumont cinema, founded its forerunner in 1832. It became the BMA in 1855. It is the main body representing doctors and other medical professionals, and acts as both trade union and upholder of professional standards. The recently-closed Worcester Infirmary where it was established stands at the bottom of Castle Street.

WORCESTER, KING CHARLES HOUSE, NEW STREET 1906 54283

The Victoria Cross was awarded to the Worcestershire Regiment nine times during the First World War. The United Kingdom's highest military award for gallantry is rather a plain affair, and therefore all the more telling. It is made of bronze from cannons captured in the Crimean War. Although it was instituted after that war, it was made retrospective to include that conflict. Almost a quarter of all VCs are awarded posthumously. It is inscribed 'For Valour'.

Among the many travellers who criss-crossed the country and reported on their journeys in centuries past, some included Worcester in their tours. Celia Fiennes arrived just in time to witness the elections of 1698. This daughter of a Cromwellian colonel seemed to enjoy the Faithful City, complimenting it on its broad streets and lofty buildings. Her contemporary Daniel Defoe was less impressed, complaining that Worcester's buildings were crowded together and its atmosphere too antique.

'The Faithful City' is a title earned by Worcester for her services to the crown during the Civil War. In fact the first and last engagements of that conflict took place at Worcester. The first, a brief but bloody Royalist victory, took place in 1642 at Powick Bridge. The last one, a full-scale battle, took place in 1651 in and around the city, ending with the Royalists in flight, their cause defeated.

WORCESTER, THE CATHEDRAL FERRY 1906 54274

WORCESTER, GHELUVELT PARK 1936 87354

William Laslett was born in Worcester in 1801. He became a barrister and the city's Member of Parliament. Laslett was eccentric, difficult, and apparently miserly. His eccentricity extended to his appearance; he walked around looking like a scarecrow. Yet this strange man gave away large sums of money and married the Bishop's daughter. He also purchased the city gaol, intending to create homes for poor citizens. Laslett Almshouses in Union Street now occupy the site.

Some Worcester streets have changed their names. Cooken Street along the south side of the Guildhall became Copenhagen Street after Nelson visited the city in 1802, commemorating a battle in which he distinguished himself. Severn Street, south of the cathedral, used to be Frog Lane, an area where many salmon fishermen lived, the fish being plentiful in days gone by. 'Lanes' often became 'Streets' when rough 'ways' and 'lanes' were first given paved surfaces.

WORCESTER, EDGAR TOWER 1910 62627A

Two Worcester girls became famous dressed as men. In the 18th century Hannah Snell enlisted in the marines and fought in India, all the time posing successfully as James Gray. She then enjoyed a brief career dressed as a marine performing on the stage. 150 years later, Vesta Tilley played a man in a long music hall career that led to marriage with an aristocrat. Vesta died a wealthy woman; poor Hannah died in poverty.

Worcester's coat of arms consists of a castle and three black pears. The former refers to the castle which stood east of the cathedral but which no longer exists. The pears are believed to have been a Worcestershire symbol since at least 1415, when Worcester bowmen adopted the symbol at the Battle of Agincourt. The fruit grows locally but is woody and only suitable for cooking, especially with red wine. It can be delicious.

When looking at medieval half-timbered buildings, take note of the number of beams visible from the street. Then look at the back; usually their number is much smaller. Oak was extremely expensive; it was therefore a sign of wealth if many beams were on public display. People passing by did not see the back, so money could be saved there without loss of prestige. Worcester has many examples in Friar Street and New Street.

**WORCESTER, LAMPS ON
THE BRIDGE 2004** W141706

Worcester City Museum houses the complete stock of a local chemist's shop, carefully displayed on the original shelves behind the original counter. The Steward family ran their shop at 27 High Street for almost one hundred years, but in 1974 its contents were sold to the museum. The building itself, with its lovely display windows, is one of more than 900 listed buildings in the city. It is now Russell and Bromley's shoe shop.

Some famous people have received the Freedom of the City: Admiral Nelson in 1802, whose carriage was dragged into Worcester by jubilant crowds; Sir Edward Elgar in 1905, when his old school friend Hubert Leicester was mayor; and in 1950 Winston Churchill, whom the mayor described as the man of the century. Churchill, whose ancestors fought for the king during the Civil War, was voted man of the century again in the millennium year.

The demolition of the cathedral's lychgate in the 1960s to make way for a new road is seen today as municipal vandalism. Such roofed entrance gateways into cemeteries were dry and sheltered spots to place a coffin before the rites of burial began. Lych is an Old English word meaning 'body' or 'corpse'. Quite a few lychgates survive, a notable example being the thatched one at Long Compton on the A3400 between Oxford and Stratford-upon-Avon.

It has been discovered recently that two famous Americans visited Worcester in 1786 to pay their respects to the Parliamentary victory at the Battle of Worcester of 1651. John Adams, who was to become the second United States president after George Washington, was serving as ambassador to Great Britain. His fellow American was the future third president, Thomas Jefferson, who was ambassador to France.

WORCESTER, THE GUILDHALL 1936 87351

Worcester Cathedral, despite its antiquity, is a New Foundation. Before the Reformation, eight English cathedrals were part of monasteries. When all monasteries were abolished, those eight cathedrals had to be re-consecrated, free of monastic taint. They therefore became known as the new foundation cathedrals.

In Worcester, the last prior of the abbey became the first dean of the cathedral. Secular and therefore non-monastic Hereford underwent no such change. It is thus an Old Foundation.

WORCESTER, ST DUNSTAN'S CRESCENT 1907 59076

WORCESTER, FRIAR STREET 1891 29321

Shakespeare used to live in Worcester! When the city's bridge was widened in 1931 the mayor was a William Shakespeare. This is a name which appears from time to time in the West Midlands. The newly-widened structure was ceremonially opened by Edward, Prince of Wales. Edward became king in 1936, but abdicated a few months later. The opening ceremony took place in the presence of Worcester's first woman mayor, Miss Diana Ogilvy.

The Dog and Duck ferry, which operated near the north end of Pitchcroft, was an important trans-shipment point for river traffic carrying cargoes to and from the region north-west of Worcester. Although the ferry no longer operates, the ferryman's cottage survives. The ferry's name derives from the unpleasant entertainment of cutting ducks' wings and placing bets on which of the dogs released from the riverbank would get to them first.

WORCESTER, THE CATHEDRAL AND THE MONASTIC RUINS 1892 29884

Worcester Cathedral appears on the old-style £20 banknote. The cathedral is closely associated with the composer, Edward Elgar, who was also shown on the note. Incidentally, the Georgian house beside the cathedral is the only privately-owned building in country ever to have featured on a British banknote.

WORCESTER, THE RIVER SEVERN FROM THE CATHEDRAL TOWER
c1960 W141077

It is rumoured that during the Second World War serious fighting broke out on the waterfront between black and white American servicemen. To preserve morale this affair was hushed up, and to help calm the situation American bandleader Glen Miller, then serving with his country's armed forces, arrived in Worcester. He was without his band. He stayed at the Star Hotel (now the Whitehouse), Foregate Street, where a Glen Miller function room commemorates his visit.

An ecological problem exists along the banks of the Severn and the Teme. The extremely tall Himalayan or Indian balsam plant threatens to swamp all other plant life. Control is extremely difficult; the best way is literally to pull it up by hand early in the year, before it flowers. It can then be left out to dry and die. This can slow its spread but cannot stop it.

The Shambles is a shopping street to the east of the High Street. Its strange name relates to 'shamels' or benches from which medieval butchers sold their wares. Before the Second World War it contained a type of shop that is noticeably absent from Worcester today: a fresh fish shop. The street name 'Shambles' is met quite often in old towns; the most famous one is situated in York.

During the Reformation a terrible event took place at the cathedral. As the abbey was closed down for ever, the monastic service books were piled up on College Green and burnt. Only one survived, an antiphoner recording the musical part of services. It is now in the cathedral library, and although a few fragments of other service books survive, the Worcester Antiphoner is the only complete pre-Reformation monastic service book in the entire country.

WORCESTER, THE CROSS 1896 38931

WORCESTER, FOREGATE STREET 1936 87350x

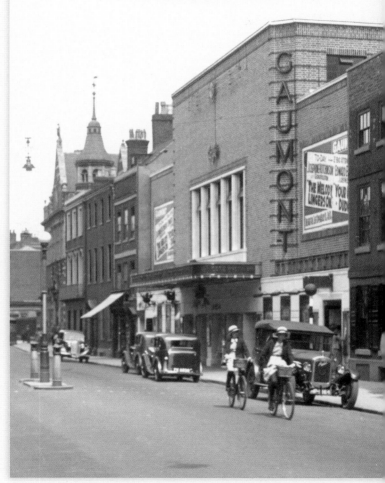

In 1582, 26-year-old Anne Hathaway found herself pregnant by 18-year-old William Shakespeare. William was legally a minor, and their marriage required permission from the Bishop of Worcester, in whose diocese they lived. The grant of this license is recorded in the diocesan registers, although the license has not survived. In Worcester, a marriage bond for £40 is preserved recording named sureties and the agreement of Anne's parents. There is no evidence that Shakespeare's parents agreed.

The Millennium Window in the cathedral south cloister consists of layers of clear glass upon which, by etching, sandblasting and drilling, significant local people over the previous millennium are depicted. They include 'Woodbine Willie', the Worcester army chaplain who brought cigarettes and spiritual comfort to the trenches during the First World War and earned the Military Cross for bravery under fire. The layers are laminated upon one another, with the exterior protected by an anti-fungal coating.

Gheluvelt Park is named after a crucial battle of the First World War in 1914. Germany was intent on reducing the Channel coast, but was held back by a small and well-trained force strung out along its lines of attack. Suddenly this line broke. Had they reached the coast the outcome of the war might have changed. 500 men from the Worcestershire Regiment fell on them and held them back long enough for the line to be reinforced.

Some of Worcester's churches are deconsecrated, used for other purposes or simply closed. In The Cross, the 18th-century church of St Nicholas is rented from the Church of England by a pub company and is called the RSVP. Its interior balcony goes right round the bar, and one can sit drinking surrounded by memorial tablets and funerary sculpture. This is because the company is not allowed to 'theme' the pub in any way.

For a brief period Worcester became part of the Italian Medici empire when, in 1520, Cardinal Giulio de'Medici was appointed Bishop of Worcester. He held the see for two years, after which he became Pope as Gregory VII. As far as we know, he never visited his English diocese.

The three bridges of central Worcester are separated from one another by approximately one hundred years. The main bridge was built in the 1780s, designed by John Gwynn of Shrewsbury. It involved extensive development of the approaches from east and west. The present railway bridge, built in 1904, replaces an earlier and more graceful bridge, the central support of which is retained. Slightly further upstream is the cable stay A-framed Sabina footbridge opened in 1992.

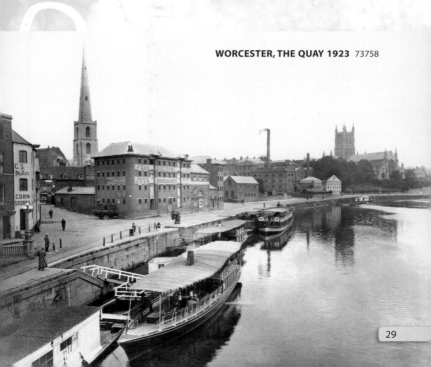

WORCESTER, THE QUAY 1923 73758

29

WORCESTER, SHIRE HALL AND VICTORIA INSTITUTE 1899 44008

One frequently comes across blocked-up house windows; Worcester has many examples. In 1696 a tax was levied on the number of windows in a house, replacing an earlier one taxing the number of hearths. The tax increased and became graduated under Pitt the younger, starting at one shilling per window. During the Napoleonic Wars the tax trebled. Blocking existing windows and reducing their number in new houses was a natural popular response.

King Charles House in New Street is shown in photograph 54283 on page 7. Nowadays the building is used as a restaurant, and there is a sign outside which reads 'From this house King Charles II escaped his enemies after the Battle of Worcester, September 3 1651'. In fact he escaped through a door at the back, which led directly on to the city walls.

The great English landscape painters Turner and Constable both visited Worcester, Constable on several occasions. He usually stayed at Diglis House, today the Diglis House Hotel, the birthplace six years before his own death of Worcester's most famous landscape artist Benjamin Williams Leader. Leader achieved Royal Academician status and used his fine technique to produce a lifelong series of idealized works, especially ones representing his native Worcestershire. These paintings made him a very rich man.

POWICK, OLD BRIDGE 1906 54290

WORCESTER, BROAD STREET
1908 59641

OLIVER'S

52

STRAW HATS & CAPS

Worcester's finest medieval timber-framed town house is the so-called Greyfriars in Friar Street, built around 1480 for a wealthy brewer. Brewing continued in the city until recent times. Lewis Clarke's brewery stood overlooking the present-day bus station, and its tall square chimney still looks down on passengers. Along the Barbourne Road stood a rival establishment, the surviving part of which has been converted to smart town houses.

In March 2004 local people celebrated a truly great sporting achievement: Best Mate, a racehorse owned by Mr Jim Lewis from Callow End, just outside the city, won the Cheltenham Gold Cup for the third successive year. This has only happened on three previous occasions, the last one being Arkle's great triumph of the 1960s.

An unusual concert hall stands within the Crowngate shopping precinct. The Huntingdon Hall was once the chapel of a non-conformist group established early in the 18th century by Selina, Countess of Huntingdon, whose thinking was much influenced by Methodism. The chapel was well attended until the 1940s, after which congregations declined. After the last service, in 1976, the ruinous building was saved through general public interest, sympathetically restored, and converted to a concert hall.

In 1858 the city received a magnificent gift in the form of a tall cast-iron fountain from Richard Padmore of the Hardy and Padmore foundry. Established alongside the Worcester to Birmingham canal by 1815, the foundry was one of Worcester's most successful businesses and found ready markets for its cast-iron street furniture. The fountain has recently been beautifully restored at a cost of £28,000, and stands once more in Cripplegate Park on the west bank.

Worcester Diocese promotes the role of women at all levels in the Church, and in the 1980s a current Worcester deaconess was a leader of the movement for women's ordination. The first women clergy were ordained at Worcester in 1994. In 2003, bishop, clergy and lay members of the Diocesan Synod agreed to propose to the General Synod of the Church of England a move towards the appointment of women bishops.

**WORCESTER, THE MALVERN HILLS FROM THE CATHEDRAL TOWER
c1960** W141080

A new tradition has begun in Worcester: the Victorian Street Fayre. The Fayre take place at the end of November as a prelude to Christmas festivities, with live entertainment, market stalls, and temporary food and drink vendors. Visitors now arrive from all over the West Midlands. However, controversy rages between those permanent shop-owners who claim they lose four days of trade and their neighbours who take the opposite view, saying that takings go up.

In front of the Shire Hall stands a statue of Queen Victoria, marking her Golden Jubilee, by local artist Sir Thomas Brock RA. Brock studied at the Worcester School of Art in Pierrepoint Street, as did his older contemporary Benjamin Williams Leader. Victoria reigned for a few months short of 64 years, the longest reign in British history; this is surprising since there were seven attempts on her life.

In 1813 the construction of a grim-looking castle was completed in Salt Lane. The lane soon became known as Castle Street. The 'castle' was in fact a new county prison, built to hold male prisoners of all categories. It was also a place of public execution, at least until 1863, with the sentence taking place above the main entrance, between the two flanking towers. After 1863, executions took place inside the prison.

The slender spire of St Andrew's Church is an 18th-century replacement for a medieval one. The church no longer survives; only its tower remains to support Nathaniel Wilkinson's spire. The whole reaches 245 ft 6 inches from the ground. Its popular name of the Glover's Needle recalls the importance of this trade to Worcester during the 18th century. In 1826, however, protectionist tariffs were removed allowing foreign gloves to be imported. The Worcester gloving industry collapsed.

The two lamps that stand in front of St George's Roman Catholic Church in Sansome Place were discovered stored away recently when the church received a restoration grant. One of the conditions of the grant was that they should be replaced in front of the building. They operate by electricity and are examples of street furniture being listed monuments.

The familiar red pillar-boxes into which we drop our letters used to be green, and their shape has been changed from time to time. The one standing by the Boer War memorial north of the cathedral is of the slim and elegant Victorian type. Some Victorian boxes are more portly. Worcester also has a rare Edward VIII pillar-box. It stands almost opposite the Northwick Cinema in the Ombersley Road.

WORCESTER, SILVER STREET c1950 W141012

WORCESTER, HIGH STREET 1931 84570

One of Worcester's most famous products is a condiment that originated in India. It was brought to England by Lord Sandys after a tour of duty in the sub-continent. Two chemists, William Perrins and John Wheeley Lea, tried to recreate its flavour, at first unsuccessfully. However, the concoction improved greatly after long maturation. We know it today as Worcestershire Sauce.

Floods are a hazard of the Severn Valley. To discover how high the waters can rise, go to the Watergate on the riverbank below the cathedral. On the wall are shown levels of exceptionally high floods. If you are six feet tall, reach up as high as you can – you will not be able to touch the most extreme marks.

WORCESTER, THE SHAMBLES c1950 W141025

WORCESTER, ANGEL PLACE c1950 W141037

Worcester's original Guildhall was a half-timbered structure described by Celia Fiennes when she visited the city in 1698 as standing on stone pillars. The northern end housed a gaol, and the gaoler in charge was also a tavern keeper. He is said to have sold his ale to his captive customers at an exorbitant price.

The new Guildhall was started in 1721 and completed in 1723. Among its functions was that of administering justice. One day in 1757, as the court was in session, violent winds sent a chimneystack crashing through the roof. Six men were killed outright and several others died later.

One day in 1892, the girls at the recently-founded Worcester High School received a surprise visit from Lewis Carroll, author of 'Alice in Wonderland'. To amuse them in the afternoon he set them a series of intriguing mathematical puzzles. This was all in accordance with headmistress Alice Otley's determination to give her pupils a rounded education.

In 1788, King George III visited Worcester. At the end of his stay, he set off northwards to visit the bishop in his palace at Hartlebury. The route led along a toll road, and King George probably had not even thought about paying. After all, he was the king! He was badly mistaken, for only on production of the appropriate toll did the gatekeeper, Robert Sleath, allow him to pass.

Two traditions are linked to Queen Elizabeth I's visit to Worcester in 1575. One is that she addressed the citizens from the balcony of the strangely isolated black-and-white building in Trinity Street known as Queen Elizabeth's House. The other is that after she saw a beautiful black pear tree, especially transplanted to her processional route by the enthusiastic citizens, she bade them add the black pears to their coat of arms.

WORCESTER, RIVER SEVERN 1904 51142

SPORTING WORCESTER

Overlooked by the cathedral, New Road in Worcester is one of the most attractive cricket grounds in the country. There has been a county side since 1847 but the present club dates from 1865. First class county status was achieved in 1899, even though the county ground was then simply three hay fields which were rented from the dean and chapter of the cathedral. Among Worcestershire's famous players have been Basil D'Oliveira, Ian Botham and Graeme Hick.

The racecourse at Worcester occupies part of Pitchcroft, which is where the Romans dumped the slag from their iron workings. The slag was removed in the 17th century, but Pitchcroft remained undeveloped, acting as a venue for fairs, circuses, military camps and musters. Horse racing is first recorded here in 1718, making it one of the oldest courses in the country. The grandstand was built in 1823, and at that time included a hotel and was operated by a local charity, St Oswald's Hospital, until the city corporation bought it in 1897, two years after buying Pitchcroft itself. The old grandstand was demolished in 1974, and its replacement opened in 1976. Racing follows National Hunt rules and covers one mile and five furlongs. Until very recently the racing at Worcester was operated by the city corporation, but since 2000 it has been run privately by Arena Leisure Services.

Worcester City Football Club was formed in 1902. The club's finest moment was in 1959, when the team beat Liverpool 2-1 in the third round of the FA Cup. They then lost to Sheffield in the 4th round, in front of a record attendance at St George's Lane of 17,042. The club's highest victory score was 18-1 against Bilston in 1931, and its heaviest defeat was 0-10 against Wellington Town in 1920.

Worcester Rugby Football Club, known as the Worcester Warriors, won promotion to the Zurich (now the Guinness) Premier League in 2004 after winning the National Division One in the 2003/04 season with a perfect record - 26 wins in 26 games.

Worcester has produced an Olympic cycling champion - Ernest Payne, who was born in the city, rode for the Worcester St Johns Cycling Club and won a gold medal in the team pursuit in the London Olympics of 1908.

WORCESTER, WORCESTERSHIRE V SURREY CRICKET MATCH 1907 59082a

QUIZ QUESTIONS

Answers on page 50.

1. Which two saints are associated with Worcester Cathedral?

2. Which medieval king was buried in Worcester Cathedral in 1216, and what is significant about his tomb?

3. Where in Worcester can you see the head of a demon pinned to the wall by his ears?

4. What is the meaning of the city's motto 'Civitas in Bello et Pace Fidelis'?

5. What is represented by the central figure surmounting the parapet of the Guildhall?

6. Which local firm made the lamps on Worcester Bridge, seen in photograph W141706 on page 14?

7. Which pub in Worcester is said to be the city's oldest?

8. The Victoria Institute contains Worcester's museum, art gallery and library and was built as a celebration of … what?

9. Whereabouts in Worcester can you see three people rising from the dead?

10. Where was Britain's first municipal hydro-electric power station opened in 1894 on the edge of Worcester, and what did the power station become when it closed down in the 1950s?

STEAD & SIMPSON

CADENA CAFÉ

FK 7585

WORCESTER, HIGH STREET c1950   W141027

RECIPE

WORCESTERSHIRE SUPPER SAVOURY

*It was in Broad Street in Worcester in 1838 that Mr Lea and Mr Perrins
first started selling their famous sauce. These amounts serve 4.*

Ingredients

4 thick slices of bread	Salt
4 slices of cheese	4 tomatoes
Mustard to taste	4 slices of bacon
Worcestershire sauce	

Preheat the oven to 200°C/400°F/Gas Mark 6.

Put a slice of cheese on each piece of bread, and spread with a little
mustard. Sprinkle a dash of Worcestershire sauce over each slice, and
add salt to taste. Slice the tomatoes and arrange on top of each slice,
then lay a slice of bacon on top. Place on a hot baking tray and bake
in the preheated oven for about 15-20 minutes, until the bacon is
cooked and crisp.

RECIPE

PEARS IN SPICED RED WINE

The species of black pear on Worcester's coat of arms is quite unpalatable in its raw state. Slow cooking in red wine is recommended - but any pears can be used in this dessert recipe, black or otherwise.

Ingredients

6 large, firm pears
300-450ml/ ½ - ¾ pint red wine
25g/1oz brown sugar

A pinch of ground cinnamon
A pinch of ground ginger

Preheat the oven to 180°C/350°F/Gas Mark 4.

Peel the pears, and stand them in a deep ovenproof dish. Mix the red wine with the brown sugar and spices, and pour it over the pears. Bake in the preheated oven for 20-30 minutes, until the pears are tender. Serve with some of the liquid spooned over each pear.

WORCESTER, THE CROSS 1923 73756

QUIZ ANSWERS

Questions on page 44.

1. St Oswald and St Wulstan (also known as St Wulfstan).

2. King John. His tomb is sited in the chancel, just before the high altar. King John was particularly fond of Worcester, and was buried in the cathedral at his own request. His tomb bears the first sculptured royal effigy in England, and is supposed to be a good likeness of the king. Other royal links with Worcester are that Henry II and his queen, Eleanor of Aquitaine, were crowned in the cathedral, and Prince Arthur, elder brother of Henry VIII and the first husband of Catherine of Aragon, was also buried there.

3. On the frontage of Worcester's impressive Guildhall in the High Street, designed by Thomas White, a local man thought to be a friend and student of Sir Christopher Wren. The carved head of a demon nailed above the door by its ears is traditionally claimed to represent Oliver Cromwell.

4. 'The City Faithful in War and in Peace.'

5. The figure on the top of the Guildhall represents Justice, because the courtroom was there.

6. Hardy and Padmore. The company specialised in finely-made cast-iron decorative products, in particular street furniture, and the reputation of its goods spread all over the world. To see some particularly lovely examples, freshly painted and gracefully poised, visit Worcester Bridge, where the parapet lamps can be inspected at close quarters.

7. The Cardinal's Hat.

8. The Victoria Institute was built to celebrate Queen Victoria's Diamond Jubilee in 1897. The statue of Queen Victoria which stands in front of the Shire Hall was erected to mark her Golden Jubilee ten years earlier.

9. In the cathedral. The Dean's chapel in the south quire transept has a 13th-century frieze of stone carvings in the spandrels of the arcading (that is, between the tops of the adjoining arches). Those on the south wall feature scenes from Judgement Day, including three members of the faithful pushing up their coffin lids as they rise from the dead. The carving can be seen in photograph 59094 below.

10. The power station was sited at Powick Bridge, and after it closed down it became a laundry.

WORCESTER, THE CATHEDRAL, RISING FROM THE DEAD 1907 59094

WORCESTER, ST JOHN'S 1925 76851

FRANCIS FRITH

PIONEER VICTORIAN PHOTOGRAPHER

Francis Frith, founder of the world-famous photographic archive, was a complex and multi-talented man. A devout Quaker and a highly successful Victorian businessman, he was philosophical by nature and pioneering in outlook. By 1855 he had already established a wholesale grocery business in Liverpool, and sold it for the astonishing sum of £200,000, which is the equivalent today of over £15,000,000. Now in his thirties, and captivated by the new science of photography, Frith set out on a series of pioneering journeys up the Nile and to the Near East.

INTRIGUE AND EXPLORATION

He was the first photographer to venture beyond the sixth cataract of the Nile. Africa was still the mysterious 'Dark Continent', and Stanley and Livingstone's historic meeting was a decade into the future. The conditions for picture taking confound belief. He laboured for hours in his wicker dark-room in the sweltering heat of the desert, while the volatile chemicals fizzed dangerously in their trays. Back in London he exhibited his photographs and was 'rapturously cheered' by members of the Royal Society. His reputation as a photographer was made overnight.

VENTURE OF A LIFE-TIME

By the 1870s the railways had threaded their way across the country, and Bank Holidays and half-day Saturdays had been made obligatory by Act of Parliament. All of a sudden the working man and his family were able to enjoy days out, take holidays, and see a little more of the world.

With typical business acumen, Francis Frith foresaw that these new tourists would enjoy having souvenirs to commemorate their days out. For the next thirty years he travelled the country by train and by pony and trap, producing fine photographs of seaside resorts and beauty spots that were keenly bought by millions of Victorians. These prints were painstakingly pasted into family albums and pored over during the dark nights of winter, rekindling precious memories of summer excursions. Frith's studio was soon supplying retail shops all over the country, and by 1890 F Frith & Co had become the greatest specialist photographic publishing company in the world, with over 2,000 sales outlets, and pioneered the picture postcard.

FRANCIS FRITH'S LEGACY

Francis Frith had died in 1898 at his villa in Cannes, his great project still growing. By 1970 the archive he created contained over a third of a million pictures showing 7,000 British towns and villages.

Frith's legacy to us today is of immense significance and value, for the magnificent archive of evocative photographs he created provides a unique record of change in the cities, towns and villages throughout Britain over a century and more. Frith and his fellow studio photographers revisited locations many times down the years to update their views, compiling for us an enthralling and colourful pageant of British life and character.

We are fortunate that Frith was dedicated to recording the minutiae of everyday life. For it is this sheer wealth of visual data, the painstaking chronicle of changes in dress, transport, street layouts, buildings, housing and landscape that captivates us so much today, offering us a powerful link with the past and with the lives of our ancestors.

Computers have now made it possible for Frith's many thousands of images to be accessed almost instantly. The archive offers every one of us an opportunity to examine the places where we and our families have lived and worked down the years. Its images, depicting our shared past, are now bringing pleasure and enlightenment to millions around the world a century and more after his death.

For further information visit: www.francisfrith.com

INTERIOR DECORATION

Frith's photographs can be seen framed and as giant wall murals in thousands of pubs, restaurants, hotels, banks, retail stores and other public buildings throughout Britain. These provide interesting and attractive décor, generating strong local interest and acting as a powerful reminder of gentler days in our increasingly busy and frenetic world.

FRITH PRODUCTS

All Frith photographs are available as prints and posters in a variety of different sizes and styles. In the UK we also offer a range of other gift and stationery products illustrated with Frith photographs, although many of these are not available for delivery outside the UK – see our web site for more information on the products available for delivery in your country.

THE INTERNET

Over 100,000 photographs of Britain can be viewed and purchased on the Frith web site. The web site also includes memories and reminiscences contributed by our customers, who have personal knowledge of localities and of the people and properties depicted in Frith photographs. If you wish to learn more about a specific town or village you may find these reminiscences fascinating to browse. Why not add your own comments if you think they would be of interest to others? See **www.francisfrith.com**

PLEASE HELP US BRING FRITH'S PHOTOGRAPHS TO LIFE

Our authors do their best to recount the history of the places they write about. They give insights into how particular towns and villages developed, they describe the architecture of streets and buildings, and they discuss the lives of famous people who lived there. But however knowledgeable our authors are, the story they tell is necessarily incomplete.

Frith's photographs are so much more than plain historical documents. They are living proofs of the flow of human life down the generations. They show real people at real moments in history; and each of those people is the son or daughter of someone, the brother or sister, aunt or uncle, grandfather or grandmother of someone else. All of them lived, worked and played in the streets depicted in Frith's photographs.

We would be grateful if you would give us your insights into the places shown in our photographs: the streets and buildings, the shops, businesses and industries. Post your memories of life in those streets on the Frith website: what it was like growing up there, who ran the local shop and what shopping was like years ago; if your workplace is shown tell us about your working day and what the building is used for now. Read other visitors' memories and reconnect with your shared local history and heritage. With your help more and more Frith photographs can be brought to life, and vital memories preserved for posterity, and for the benefit of historians in the future.

Wherever possible, we will try to include some of your comments in future editions of our books. Moreover, if you spot errors in dates, titles or other facts, please let us know, because our archive records are not always completely accurate—they rely on 140 years of human endeavour and hand-compiled records. You can email us using the contact form on the website.

Thank you!

For further information, trade, or author enquiries
please contact us at the address below:

**The Francis Frith Collection, Oakley Business Park,
Wylye Road, Dinton, Wiltshire SP3 5EU.**
Tel: +44 (0)1722 716 376 Fax: +44 (0)1722 716 881
e-mail: sales@francisfrith.co.uk **www.francisfrith.com**